If Not You,
Who?

If Not You, Who?

Who?

Cracking the Code of Employee Disengagement

By

Jill Christensen

Vertex Learning, LLC

Washington DC • Atlanta • Denver • St. Louis • Dayton

www.vertexlearning.com

For more information on Vertex Learning Educational Research, Publishing and Consulting, visit our website at www.vertexlearning.com.

ISBN: 978-1-4951-6924-3

Library of Congress Cataloging-in-Publication Data

Christensen, Jill

If Not You, Who? Cracking the Code of Employee Disengagement.

Printed and bound in the United States of America.

Discounts on this title may be available at the author's discretion available in bulk orders: Contact Vertex Learning at info@vertexlearning.com or 240 640 1212.

Artwork by: Hollie Shivers

CONTENTS

ACKNOWLEDGMENTS

As a first-time author, I can truly say that the book-writing journey is incredible. It takes a village to raise a child and it also takes a village to write a book. I had helpers, coaches, tutors, teachers, guides, editors, mentors, and supporters. Everyone played a powerful role.

- To my Father, Robert, who taught me the values of knowledge and hard work. To my Mother, Brenda, who taught me the values of being genuine and real, and to never ever give up on my dreams. This combination is powerful, so thank you. I hit the parent lottery.

- To my amazing Sister, Kim, and my friends. You support me, encourage me, inspire me, and lift me up. This is why you are in my life. I'll only surround myself with self-confident, courageous, present, and optimistic people, who are role models for the teachings in this book. I'm grateful for you.

- To my guides, both here are afar. My magical book team helped make this possible - God, my 13 Helpers, Susan March, Melodie Matice, Judith Briles, Jerry Maglio, Jennifer Piehl, Alfonzo Porter, and Vertex Learning. You taught me the ropes and stood by my side every step of the way. You are talented and generous beyond belief.

- To Starbucks, for allowing me to sit in your stores for weeks on end, refilling my Green Iced Tea for free, as I wrote this book.
- To every supervisor I've ever had. I've learned from both the strong ones and the weak ones. Thank you for seeing my potential, helping me grow, and challenging me.
- To every person I've ever supervised. You taught me how to be strong and courageous. You made us look good. Leading you was a privilege and I hope I added to your life in a big way. You added to mine.
- To the companies and clients who have entrusted me with your success. It's through my life's work in your halls that I know what I know, am who I am, and do what I do.

This book is the beginning of me realizing my purpose in life; of me putting my piece of the puzzle in place. Thank you from the bottom of my heart for believing in me. You are all Champions in my eyes and I'm honored to have you in my life.

CHAPTER 1

The Truth

There seems to be some perverse human characteristic that likes to make easy things difficult.
—Warren Buffett, Most Successful Investor of the 20th Century

The stakes are high.

You are the coach of a five-man basketball team battling against another team. But this isn't just any game. It's the Olympics and it's all for the glory. You are leading the team who is gunning for Gold in the men's basketball final. Hundreds of thousands of sports fanatics—representing virtually every country in the world—hover above their colorful stadium seats shouting with all their might in the hopes of inspiring your team to victory. You are about to begin the fight of your life ... battling for the title of "best in the world."

As the ball is tossed in the air at center court, one of your star players grabs it and races down the wooden planks as fast as he can, gunning for the competitor's net. Just imagine, three of your five starting players are standing at center court waving to their family and friends in the stands. Your final starting player is watching ESPN SportsCenter on a TV in the locker room as he sips lime-green Gatorade and roots for the opposing team.

Is it real? Absolutely! Leaders, this is your workforce today!

Houston, We Have a Problem

According to Gallup, 87 percent of global workers and 70 percent of American workers are "disengaged" from their jobs and "emotionally disconnected" from their workplaces. The cost to the U.S. economy is $500 billion per year and trillions to the global economy. Have you calculated your share?

Why should the employee disengagement crisis keep you up at night? Your personal success and your company's success hinge on your ability to engage your workforce.

> **employee engagement**
> [em-ploi-ee en-gage-munt]
> *noun*
> 1. the emotional commitment the
> employee has to the organization and its
> goals.

There is no getting around the fact that there is a direct correlation between employee engagement and profitability. The most successful companies in the world have the highest levels of employee engagement and realize other important benefits, including:

- Increased employee productivity and customer satisfaction.

- Increased company performance and profitability.
- Increased employee retention.
- Decreased safety incidents, theft, absenteeism, and quality defects.

Engaged employees go the extra mile and do everything they can to ensure the company succeeds. That extra effort pays enormous dividends.

Mark Crowley is the author of *Lead From the Heart: Transformational Leadership for the 21st Century*. In a recent article in *FastCompany* magazine, he wrote:

> Gallup's report shows that organizations in the top tier of engagement outperform their peers by 147 percent in earnings per share and have a 90 percent better growth trend than their competition.

It Really is Madness and March Has Nothing To Do with It

What do disengaged employees do with their time? They play online games, surf Internet sites, nod off, and heat-up the social media airwaves with friends, family members, and co-workers. The Chicago outplacement firm Challenger, Gray & Christmas issued a press release based in part on U.S. Bureau of Labor Statistics data. The firm purported that employers could lose up to $1.9 billion in wages due to the 60 million American workers who devour the NCAA men's basketball tournament, affectionately known as March Madness.

THE TRUTH

Disengaged employees offer the greatest untapped potential for your business to improve its profitability and performance. Period.

With these realities in mind, it stands to reason that disengaged employees offer the greatest untapped potential for your business to improve its profitability and performance. Your business will never win Olympic Gold in your industry if you do not step-up and awaken this untapped potential.

THREE CATEGORIES OF WORKER ENAGAGEMENT

- **Engaged:** Employees work with passion and feel a profound connection to their company. They drive innovation and move the organization forward.

- **Disengaged:** Employees are sleepwalking through their workday, putting time—but not energy or passion—into their work.

- **Actively Disengaged:** Employees aren't just unhappy at work; they're busy acting out their unhappiness. Every day, these workers undermine what their engaged co-workers accomplish.

Why You Exist ... I Know, This is Big ... Right?

The world is a giant puzzle, made up of seven billion people. Therefore, seven billion unique pieces. You are one piece of the puzzle and your piece is like no other. If you leave this world without having put your piece in place, you've not only robbed yourself, but you've also robbed the world of your gift.

Owning up to the responsibilities you have to the Earth—and the people you share it with—and making a difference in this world is the real definition of success. Nothing matters more and nothing will make you feel more fulfilled in life. It's why you were created. It's why you exist. It's a part of your purpose.

THE TRUTH

If you leave this world without having put your piece of the puzzle in place, you've not only robbed yourself, but you've also robbed the world of your gift.

We all have responsibilities at home, in our community, and in our workplace. As a leader at work, one of your main responsibilities ... your piece of the puzzle ... is to create an environment that people love where they can soar, so your company meets or exceeds its goals. You owe it to employees to create an environment that excites them, lights them up inside, and inspires them to give their all; and then some.

Step-Up or Step Aside

What is your role as a leader as it relates to employee engagement? In one word: Everything! The reason employee engagement initiatives have failed for the past 30 years is because they are created as stand-alone programs with few linkages to the actual business; therefore, they are not a priority. Historically, employee engagement has been the "program du jour." In order for employee engagement to soar in your company, your role is to partner with other leaders to *"own it" and make it a priority*.

Everything in business rises and falls as a result of leadership. If a company has high levels of employee engagement and meets or exceeds its goals, odds are there's a great leader or leadership team that has owned up to its responsibilities.

You may be thinking: *that's not fair.*

- Why is it all about me? If every employee simply "owned" their engagement, we wouldn't have this problem.

- Why aren't employees taking responsibility for their attitude and getting with the program?

Both excellent questions that create multiple responses.

When you are responsible for other people at work, you've graduated from being an individual performer into being a leader. Step up and own it, or step aside.

While employees are a part of the equation, consider this. The truth is that although every employee may be doing his/her best with good intent, many people are complicated, lack self-confidence, and live in fear. Employees are also incredibly distracted both at work and at home. Is this really who you want to rely on to help improve your disengagement crisis?

I didn't think so! Leaders, if you really understood the importance of culture on your bottom line, you'd "own it" and stop outsourcing it to Human Resources. Take it upon yourself to own employee engagement and create an environment people love where they can soar, and you will see a measurable change in your workforce. Your employees will become more confident, courageous, attentive, and engaged. Consequently, your business performance and profitability will increase.

You are in a leadership role for a reason: to ensure your company succeeds. If you don't think you have what it takes to lead an employee engagement revolution in your workplace, then put together a game plan to get back into the ranks of individual performers—people who do not supervise others. When you are responsible for other people at work, you've graduated from being an individual performer into being a leader ... a Champion. Step up and own it, or step aside.

Trust Me, It Works

I saw this phenomenon play out at Avaya, a global provider of next-generation business collaboration and communications solutions. I led their global Internal Communications organization. The leadership team understood the ramifications of having a disengaged workforce, so we implemented many of the concepts contained in the pages within *If Not You, Who?*

Leaders didn't ask disengaged employees to come to work tomorrow engaged. Leaders believed that if they created an environment people love where they could soar, employee engagement and profits would rise. They were right!

We implemented a global strategic plan within Avaya to crack the code of employee disengagement and in two years we:

- Drove a six- to 16-point increase in three employee engagement survey categories: strategy buy-in, confidence in senior leaders, and open and honest communications.

- Moved the overall Corporate Employee Engagement score from 51 to 62 percent (a two-percentage point increase is considered "statistically significant").

- Realized a 26 percent rise in Avaya's stock price.

My guess is that if you realized similar measurable results in your company, you'd be viewed as a Champion, so keep reading!

I'm Onboard. Now What?

So what's a leader to do? Mike Dooley, author of *Infinite Possibilities,* says, "You are not meant to bear that which you find unpleasant; you are meant to change it."

Change it? By ordering employees to be engaged? By stopping employees from filling out March Madness college basketball brackets? By eliminating break rooms and ping pong tables? Not by a longshot.

Employees want to be trusted and they don't want to be micromanaged. They want to have autonomy in their day, knowing that it's OK to submit their basketball bracket during work hours, as long as they also do the work that is expected of them—as long as they place their piece in the puzzle.

You are going to change it by doing two things:

- championing a four-step process; and

- modifying your behaviors in the workplace.

It really is that simple.

To crack the code of employee disengagement, I could give you a list of 20 traits that all leaders need to possess. I also could have developed multiple employee engagement solutions for different geographical regions, ages, sexes, tenures, and blah, blah, blah. However, I didn't do that. Why? Because it's not that complicated.

Two of my takeaways from decades in Corporate America, working for global Fortune 500 companies in seven different industries, are:

- People make things a lot harder than they have to be.

- People are basically the same everywhere in the world because we are all human. Cultures and languages may differ, but people are people. Yes, even the Millennials.

Because people are basically the same everywhere in the world, there's one solution to improve employee disengagement and your profitability—whether you are a two-person company in India or a 300,000-person company in the United States. Your bottom line: there are four **things** you need to **do** and four **ways** you need to **be.** It's that basic.

THE TRUTH

People make things a lot harder than they have to be and people are basically the same everywhere in the world. Yes, even the Millennials.

Go Forth and Conquer, Champ!

Tackle this issue with passion and make your employee disengagement crisis as big a priority as whether your new product line is meeting its revenue targets in Europe. When you do, you will realize greater success in virtually every area of your business and you will have cracked the code of employee disengagement. Kapow!

Now let's blow the doors off this barn and make you look like the Champion you are ...

PART ONE
Four Things You Need to Do

CHAPTER 2

Get the Right Person in Every Chair

I am convinced that nothing we do is more important than hiring and developing people. At the end of the day you bet on people, not on strategies.
—Lawrence Bossidy, ex-CEO of GE Credit Corp, Allied Signal/Honeywell

Engaging employees starts with hiring the right ones in the first place. This applies to both individual contributors and people who manage employees (people managers). At the end of the day, the wrong person cannot be engaged regardless of how amazing your work environment is.

How do you get the right person in every chair? You accomplish this by being incredibly selective in the hiring process. You must hire people who are both a good fit for the job and a good fit for the culture you are creating.

WANTED: People Who Believe What Your Company Believes

Simon Sinek, author and creator of the third most-viewed TEDx video, shares,

The goal is not to hire people who need a job. The goal is to hire people who believe what you believe. If you hire people just because they can do the job, they'll work for your money, but if you hire people who believe what you believe, they'll give you blood, sweat, and tears.

How do you distinguish between the two, you ask? State what your company does—and its purpose and values—in the job ad. Incorporate questions about values in the recruiter's pre-screen phone call and drill the candidate about values in a face-to-face interview. Make it clear that the only person who will succeed in the role is someone who can do the job and whose values are completely aligned with the company's beliefs.

THE TRUTH

The goal is not to hire people who need a job. The goal is to hire people who believe what your company believes.

When you have employees in your company whose values are not aligned with your company's values, you will have engagement issues. When engagement issues are not addressed, your high performers may leave, which is a very costly proposition. Studies show that the cost of losing an employee can range from tens of thousands of dollars to one and one-half times annual salary—in specialty positions, it can run many times higher. Outside of the decline in productivity when you lose an engaged employee, your internal employee morale nose-dives and over-all customer satisfaction can take a hit.

WANTED: People Managers Who Inspire. Others Need Not Apply.

Dr. Jim Harter, Gallup's chief scientist of workplace management and well-being, has been at the forefront of employee engagement research since 1997; initiating the first "State of the American Workplace" study. Marc Crowley, a workplace thought leader, sat down with Harter to ask what is causing employees to disengage and under-commit themselves at work.

In Crowley's article, referred to in the previous chapter, Harter says,

> Companies must ensure everyone selected for a leadership position has the talent to be an inspiring and effective manager. You can't afford to get this wrong, or it's an uphill battle. Workplaces have paid a lot of attention to process and much less to people. Too often, employees are given managerial roles tied to success in a previous role, or as a reward for their tenure.

How do you gauge a person's ability to inspire others? You have to observe them. You need to ask yourself questions like:

- *Does this person inspire you?*
- *If he/she was leading you into a dark basement would you follow with trust and confidence, and even be slightly excited?*
- *Or, would you be paralyzed by fear?*

In the face-to-face interview, delve into a person's willingness, confidence, and ability to lead others. One of the most common and consistent hiring mistakes is failing to speak with several people who the candidate has supervised in the past. Past behavior is an extraordinary predictor of future behavior. Don't gloss over it.

THE TRUTH

Past behavior is an extraordinary predictor of future behavior. Don't gloss over it.

There's another criteria when hiring people who manage others. Your company is embarking on a new way of "How we do things here." In this new environment, your people managers will play a critical role in helping to turn the tide of employee engagement, as they are the frontline to your employees. Therefore, every people manager must be passionate about driving and leading change, and know what's expected of them.

Their leadership will make or break your ability to re-engage employees.

I know that many people don't like change. However, if your leadership team acts as role models, starts doing things differently, and shares the positive results with your people managers, they'll get onboard. How do I know? I know from a lifetime of experience.

Cat Food Isn't the Solution

My father worked for IBM his entire career. In the 1970s, people said the acronym IBM stood for "I've Been Moved" because workers were transferred often. He was a part of this era, so we moved every five years. Our first move was from New York to Texas. IBM put all of our family's belongings in an Allied moving truck and Dad, Mom, Sister Kim, and I flew to Texas with our pets under our airplane seats. The only things we carried with us were a few days' worth of clothing and cat food, so we wouldn't have to immediately find a store when we landed.

When we got to Dallas, we rented a car and began the drive to Arlington. As I looked out the car window at the tumbleweed from the back seat, I thought about how I had been picked up and moved across the country to an unfamiliar place. I left behind the home I grew up in, my friends, my school, and many extended family members. I was so stressed about the change that I reached into my mom's large purse, pulled out a Ziploc bag, and began eating dry cat food. If that isn't the definition of emotional eating, I don't know what is!

THE TRUTH

As a leadership team, act as role models—start doing things differently, share the positive results with your people managers, and they'll get onboard.

But within weeks of our move, I saw many positive results. I loved the sunshine, my new yellow bedroom, my teachers, the rodeo, and my season pass to Six Flags amusement park. So when Dad came home one day and announced that we were moving to Michigan, I had a very different reaction. I didn't eat cat food. I had evidence that the change to Texas yielded positive results, so I trusted that the change to Michigan would yield positive results as well. I was right.

More Truth and This One May Hurt

We've reviewed the importance of getting the right person in every chair, but what if you already have employees in chairs who do not believe what your company believes, or if you have people managers in chairs who are not strong leaders and cannot inspire others? You know you do—every company does—so hold onto the chair you are sitting in, as I'm about to share more truth, which you must embrace and act upon if you are going to build an engaged workforce.

In a world where results matter, holding people accountable is a must. When people are held accountable, it builds trust, creates strong teams, fewer balls are dropped, and it sends the message that mediocrity is not OK. When people are not held accountable, it acts like a cancer in your organization ... ravishing the workplace. It breaks down trust, breaks down teams, balls are dropped, and a message is sent that mediocrity is OK.

Joseph A. Michelli, author of *The Starbucks Experience*, writes,

> The Starbucks Experience is a commitment to the shared good of all employees and customers. It happens by creating systems to hold leadership and staff accountable for that commitment, sharing the reward of hard work, and encouraging profitability.

There is nothing more demoralizing to an employee than a management team who allows a person to stay on a team who is not pulling their weight, who has a toxic attitude, or who can't effectively manage others. Regardless of the person's issue, this behavior is like a cancer. The only way to stop the cancer from spreading or stop its effects is to develop the employee. If that does not work, terminate the perpetrator.

Sometimes a Person's Best is Not Good Enough

While everyone is doing his/her best and is of good intent (no one wakes up in the morning and says, "I'm going to under-perform today and fail to achieve my goals"), sometimes a person's best is not good enough.

Sports teams cut people all of the time, which is why the notion of an employee suing a company for wrongful discharge when their performance is low dumbfounds me. Can you imagine if Peyton Manning sued the Indianapolis Colts for releasing him from the team in 2012?

To give you some context, Manning is a NFL quarterback who led the Colts to eight division championships, three conference championships, and one Super Bowl championship. His five NFL most valuable players honors are a league record, he was the most valuable player of Super Bowl XLI, has been named to 14 Pro Bowls, has 13 seasons with 4,000 passing yards, and is the Colts' all-time leader in passing yards and touchdown passes. In 2009, he was named the best player in the NFL and *Sports Illustrated* named him the NFL player of the decade for the 2000s.

Manning didn't sue the Colts for wrongful discharge because he's a winner, a Champion. As a Champion, he understands that although his talents served the Colts well in the past, they didn't think his talents would serve them well in the future. He was released from the team. It was completely within the Colts' rights to make that call.

However, true Champions (high performers) are few and far between. Approximately 10 percent of employees are high performers, 80 percent are in the middle or average, and 10 percent are below average or mediocre.

THE TRUTH

The majority of your employees are not high performers and they don't think like Champions. Therefore, you are going to wind up with people in chairs who don't belong there.

While these numbers may be controversial to some, there's a truth here that you need to understand and embrace. The majority of your employees are not high performers and they don't think like Champions. Therefore, you are going to wind up with people in chairs who are below average ... mediocre ... and who are not helping to move your company forward.

> **mediocre**
> [mee-dee-o-ker]
> *adjective*
> 1. not very good.

As I said before, everyone is doing their best (as they define it), but sometimes a person's best isn't good enough. I can tell you from experience that when you have a person in a role who is under performing, everyone around that person knows it and does one of two things. They choose to stay, picking up the slack for the under-performer, and become resentful and disengaged. Or, they choose to leave, emailing and/or texting their resignation notice.

Often, it's not the employees in the middle or at the bottom who resign. It's the Champions, your high performers. The people who have confidence and courage, and who know that they possess valuable skills and can easily get hired elsewhere—the ones you want to keep.

According to Judith Briles, author of *Stabotage!*,

> When action is taken to alter a negative workplace, morale, loyalty, and productivity increase; teams are strengthened; stress levels are reduced; turn-over decreases; management is viewed as proactive; and money is saved.

It bears repeating: There is nothing more demoralizing to an employee than a management team who allows a person to stay on a team who is not pulling their weight, who has a toxic attitude, or who can't effectively manage others. Regardless of the person's issue, this behavior is like a cancer. The only way to stop the cancer from spreading or stop its effects is to develop the employee. If that does not work, remove the perpetrator.

There is nothing more demoralizing to an employee than a management team who allows a person to stay in their role, who is not pulling their weight, who has a toxic attitude, or who can't effectively manage others.

Document, Document, Document

To that end, you need a performance management process that enables you to document, so when you do course-correct and terminate underperformers, you protect yourself against a potential lawsuit. You need to be able to prove—*in writing*—that the employee:

1. Was aware of, and agreed to, his/her goals and what is expected.
2. Was told exactly how he/she is falling short of the goals, with concrete examples and feedback from other employees.
3. Was put on a development plan with specific actions meant to help the employee improve.
4. Failed to improve in the stated timeframe, and the implications the failure had on his/her immediate team and the company overall.

All of the steps above must be in writing and signed by the employee. If the situation improves but other issues appear, continue to document. If new issues are rectified, document that the employee has improved and is no longer on a development plan. In light of all this documentation, you still may lose a lawsuit, but at least you will go to the table armed with evidence to make your best case in the hopes of protecting your company's assets.

Firing an employee is never easy, but it's usually the best thing for everyone involved. The employee wasn't a good fit for you, but that does not mean they are a poor fit for every company. Rectify your hiring mistakes by releasing people who are not doing what they are being paid to do.

Do your company and the underperforming employee a favor: give the person honest feedback, and replace him/her with someone who can do the job and who believes what your company believes.

If this makes you feel better, every employee who I chose to fire or who I was told to fire (yes, people managers are often told who to fire) didn't stay unemployed for long. They all landed a great job in another company and are thriving. Do you know who else is thriving? Peyton Manning moved from the Colts to the Denver Broncos, quickly becoming a beloved member of the community. In his first four years at the helm, Manning consecutively brought his team to the playoffs and was victorious in Super Bowl 50. It works out OK, trust the process.

In order for your company to succeed, you must have the right person in every chair. No exceptions. Champions know this and have the courage to act when they see a cancer amongst them. You are a Champion, right? I thought so.

WHAT A CHAMPION WOULD DO NEXT

Partner with your Human Resources organization or contact to conduct an audit and implement changes:

- Do your open job ads state what your company believes in?
- Do you ask candidates if there is alignment in beliefs during the recruiter's pre-screen phone call?
- Do your hiring managers know to drill the candidate about beliefs in the face-to-face interview?
- Do your hiring managers know to speak to several people who the individual managed in the past (if it's a people manager position).
- Do your hiring managers (as well as anyone else on the interview team) use open-ended, behavior-based questions in their interviewing process?
- Do your hiring managers know to rate people honestly and document all performance conversations, putting low performers on a development plan and terminating low performers who do not improve?
- Hold people managers accountable by ensuring that anyone who leads others has a "people manager" goal in his/her objectives. If your employees don't have goals, they will once you finish reading chapter three.
- Start doing things differently, share the positive results with your people managers, and they'll embrace the change ... I promise.

Get the right person in every chair and you are one step ahead.

CHAPTER 3

Create a Line of Sight Between What Employees Do Day-to-Day and the Company's Goals

You reach a point where you don't work for money.
—Walt Disney, Entertainment Visionary

In order to be engaged, employees need to see that what they do matters.

- They need to see where they fit into the puzzle ... the bigger picture of where your company is going.
- They need to see that they are a critical piece.
- They need to see that their purpose and your company's purpose are aligned.
- They need to see that they are contributing and the business will not be as successful without them.

As a business leader, it's your job to help them on this journey.

Success Factors, a leader in cloud-based Human Capital Management software, reports that studies show a dramatic increase in both worker and business performance when an organization effectively sets—and closely ties—individual employee goals to the company's overall strategy. Yet amazingly, a mere seven percent of employees today fully understand their company's business goals and strategies, and what's expected of them in order to help achieve company business goals.

THE TRUTH

People are not motivated by external rewards. They are motivated by the deeply human need to direct their life, and do better for ourselves and for the world.

Business strategist and author Daniel Pink says,

> People are not motivated by external rewards. They are motivated by the deeply human need to direct their life, and do better for themselves and the world.

This reality holds true for all of your current employees, regardless of their age, and especially for the

Millennials—those born between 1980 and 2000.
Multinational professional services firm Price Waterhouse
Coopers estimates that by 2020, Millennials will form
50 percent of the global workforce. Far more vocal than
Traditionalists, Baby Boomers, and Generation X, they
communicate their hopes, dreams, and wishes.
Millennials refuse to be another cog in the wheel and if
you don't give them what they need, they'll simply quit.
Imagine the impact on your business if half of your
workforce left simply because they are disengaged.

Generations in the Workforce
- Traditionalists: Born Before 1946
- Baby Boomers: Born Between 1946 and 1964
- Generation X: Born Between 1965 and 1979
- Millennials/Generation Y: Born Between 1980
  and 2000

One Millennial shared his views in a post within
Entrepreneur.com:

> I'm 30, an ex-corporate executive at
> Blackberry and now the CEO of a business-
> collaboration start-up. I know a thing or
> two about Millennials, so I'd like to explain
> what's going on. We've been labeled the
> 'entitlement generation' and have been
> called many things, with varying degrees of
> accuracy. The bottom line, however, is that
> we don't have the same value-set as our
> parents or grandparents. A lifelong career

with a work/life balance may have been a goal for their generations, but isn't ours. We want purpose. We want meaning.

TRUTH

Millennials don't want to be another cog in the wheel. They want purpose. They want meaning.

When employees feel a sense of purpose, they are more engaged and productive, which translates into your company's strategy being executed more quickly. All the more reason why every employee in your company needs to understand why it exists and how what they do day-to-day contributes to that purpose. When this link is missing, employees feel adrift, like a castaway on a rickety wooden raft floating aimlessly in the ocean.

I Can See Clearly Now

In *The Starbucks Experience*, author Joseph A. Michelli writes,

Often, employees do not see how their efforts help the organization succeed. Similarly, employees cannot see how the businesses' success relates to them. The trick for management, therefore, is to get employees to see the bigger picture and understand that small components of their day-to-day tasks actually have a transformational impact on customers and people with whom they work, not to mention on the company's overall mission and reputation.

If employees do not understand the big picture and see how their piece adds to and completes the puzzle, they will be disengaged. They will arrive at work every day and simply go through the motions, doing what they have to do to get by. Imagine the negative impact this has on productivity, customer satisfaction, absenteeism, quality defects, and most importantly, and the granddaddy of them all: profitable revenue growth.

In order to be engaged, employees need to see that what they do matters.

- They need to see where they fit into the puzzle—the bigger picture of where your company is going;
- They need to see that they are a critical piece;
- They need to see that their purpose and your company's purpose are aligned; and
- They need to see that they are contributing and your company will not be as successful without them.

As a leader, it's your job to create this clear line of sight.

Do you know what happens when there is no clear line of sight for employees? Mayhem happens.

An Unforgettable Experience; Just for You

My father served in the U.S. Navy, so he is an adventurer and can captain a 40-foot sailboat. He also loves to travel and explore new places, so he came home one day with a glossy magazine from the Moorings, a yacht charter and sailboat rental company. The words, "An Unforgettable Experience, Just for You," were splashed on the brochure cover along with a picture of a beautiful tanned woman lying on the front of the boat drinking a Piña Colada.

Inside of the brochure were pictures of some of the most breath-taking islands and beaches I had ever seen. The water was as blue as a turquoise stone and you could tell that the sand would feel like baby powder beneath your feet. One picture showed a man grilling fresh shrimp on the sailboat's BBQ grill as he was serenaded by a steel band playing in the distance on shore. It looked magical.

Dad said to the entire family, "I think we should charter a boat in the British Virgin Islands for a week and sail the open waters as a family. What do you think?" I jumped up in excitement and said, "Count me in. This trip looks amazing!"

Six months later our plane landed in Tortola, where we began our journey. We were escorted from the marina to our boat, which would be home for the next seven days. I was on cloud nine...

purpose
[pur-puh-s]
noun
1. the reason for which something exists.

As soon as Dad boarded the boat he called a meeting in the cockpit. "Kim, you are going to work the sails and ropes. Jill, you'll be our cook and will catch fish. Brenda, you'll clean the boat and keep water off the deck at all times. Steve, you are responsible for the anchor, the dingy, and finding moorings." I said, "Hold on ... what is all this? I thought I signed up for a vacation. The brochure shows me laying on the boat's bow drinking Piña Coladas. I thought I was in for an unforgettable experience!"

Well I was, but it wasn't the unforgettable experience I had imagined. During that week, I worked 100 times harder than I ever had at work. If you've boated on the open ocean for longer than an afternoon, you know what I'm talking about.

We were sunburned. Our dinghy's motor broke two days into the trip, so we had to row every time we needed to get to shore. When we were in the dinghy we were surrounded by hundreds of five-foot-long tarpon fish trying to leap into our raft in the darkness of night. Our cramped sleeping quarters were so hot that I slept on the boat deck. Our electric anchor line broke, so we had to haul up the anchor by hand. We encountered a storm and our boat was blown around and around a mooring 1,000 times in one night. Our winch went overboard, so we did not have a way to pull in or let out the boat's ropes. These are the highlights.

Needless to say, by day two, I was completely disengaged. Why? The trip's goals did not align with my individual goals, and I did not see how cooking meals and catching fish added value. I boarded the boat looking for rest and relaxation. I wanted to eat conch fritters and plantains in the local restaurants. Bottom line, my father had made a bad hiring decision—me.

However, my sister Kim was not disengaged. Her goals aligned perfectly with the trip's goals, and she felt incredibly valuable every time she worked the sails and ropes. She boarded the boat looking for a challenging adventure and that's exactly what she experienced.

When an employee sees that their purpose is aligned with your company's purpose, and what they do is contributing to your success, they'll be engaged. If the alignment is missing, they'll be disengaged. How do you give employees a clear line of sight between their job and the company's purpose? By ensuring you have goal alignment.

We're Heading to the Left. Yes, All of Us, Together

Simply put, goal alignment involves ensuring that every person in your company from top to bottom is doing work that supports the company's goals. It involves getting everyone to march in the same direction. I don't care if you have two people in your company or 300,000 ... every employee must have goals that support the company's goals.

How do you give employees a clear line of sight between their job and the company's purpose? Goal alignment.

The goal alignment process works like this:

1. The company's goals are set for the upcoming year (three to five maximum).
2. The President or CEO writes his/her goals in support of the company's goals.
3. Each Executive Team Member writes his/her goals in support of the President or CEO's goals.
4. Each Vice President writes his/her goals in support of their Executive Team Member's goals.
5. Each Director writes his/her goals in support of their Vice President's goals.
6. Each Senior Manager writes his/her goals in support of their Director's goals.
7. Each Manager writes his/her goals in support of their Senior Manager's goals.
8. Each Management Associate or Support Staff member writes his/her goals in support of their Manager's goals.

This process should take place three months prior to the start of your company's fiscal year and it is fluid. If there is a major event during the fiscal year that necessitates your company moving in a different direction, then goals must be rewritten.

When this process is complete, every employee in the organization has goals that support their chain of command all the way up to the CEO, and that support the company's goals. This is how you ensure that everyone is marching in the same direction and only doing work that supports the company's purpose.

This is also how employees see line of sight between what they do every day and where the company is going. This is how employees see that what they do matters. This is how employees see where they fit into the puzzle—the bigger picture of where your company is going. This is how employees see that they are a critical piece—they are adding value—and that the business will not be as successful without them. This is how you engage a workforce.

Be SMART

The November 1981 issue of *Management Review* published a paper by George T. Doran called *There's a S.M.A.R.T. Way to Write Management's Goals and Objectives*. It discussed the importance of objectives revealed through Doran's SMART model. Decades later, the SMART methodology is so effective that it is still widely used in companies today.

Each company and individual goal should be:

- **Specific:** Target a specific area for improvement.

- **Measurable:** Quantify, or at least suggest, an indicator of progress.
- **Assignable:** Specify who will do it.
- **Realistic:** State what results can realistically be achieved, given available resources.
- **Time-related:** Specify when the result(s) can be achieved.

Example of a SMART Goal: *The Asia Pacific sales team will improve customer satisfaction ratings by three percent by the end of the calendar year to 78 percent, as determined by the annual customer satisfaction survey.*

Annual Performance Reviews? Not

Checking progress toward goals once a year will not help create an engaged workforce, and ensure employees are on track to meet or exceed objectives. To that end, companies need to rethink the traditional annual performance review process. Regular checkpoints need to occur between people managers and employees, so employees are reminded that what they do day-to-day matters and can make course corrections in real time.

 **THE TRUTH**

Checking progress toward goals once a year will not help create an engaged workforce, and ensure people are on track to meet or exceed objectives.

Several global powerhouses have turned the traditional annual performance review process on its side. Consulting firm Accenture eliminated annual performance reviews for its 330,000 workers, following in the footsteps of Microsoft, which eliminated its ranking system. Accenture's system calls for informal reviews that can be given at the manager's discretion. At Gap, managers have monthly conversations with workers, and Google and Yahoo have opted for quarterly reviews.

You can't expect employees to be engaged when they have one conversation a year with their manager about their performance and their role in the company's success. In order for employees to see the line of sight between what they do every day and the company's purpose, people managers must conduct formal (weekly, monthly, or quarterly) conversations with their people about their performance and document those conversations in writing. In addition, people managers should give employees informal feedback in the moment when an employee is doing something well or poorly.

THE TRUTH

To engage your workforce and meet or exceed your goals, you must get everyone in your company marching in the same direction toward a common goal.

Employees need to be frequently reminded that by putting their piece of the puzzle in place, they are helping the company achieve its goals, and it could not be done without them.

- Show them that their contributions matter. Then stand by and watch.
- Watch them be more productive.
- Watch them have more passion.
- Watch them be more creative.
- And watch your employee engagement needle, as it will be on the rise.

WHAT A CHAMPION WOULD DO NEXT

- Partner with your Human Resources department or person to:
    - Implement goal alignment in your company.
    - Ensure all goals are written following the SMART methodology.
    - Shift to quarterly or monthly formal performance reviews.
    - Encourage people managers to give informal, real-time feedback in the moment when an employee is doing something well or poorly.
- Engage your Internal Communications department or person to:
    - Focus on goal alignment—and its benefits—in employee communications.
    - Attribute "business wins" to having an aligned team who is marching in the same direction.
- Refrain from judging Millennials. They want what everyone wants: purpose and meaning in their work. Unlike other generations, they are more willing to speak up and tell you what they need to be engaged. What more could you ask for?

Get the right person in every chair, and create a line of sight between what employees do day-to-day and the company's goals, and you are two steps ahead.

CHAPTER 4

Build a Two-Way Communication Culture

It's about communication. It's about honesty. It's about treating people in the organization as deserving to know the facts. You don't give them half the story. You don't hide the story. You treat them as true equals, and you communicate, and you communicate, and you communicate.

—Louis V. Gerstner, Jr., ex-CEO, IBM

Communicating openly and honestly, and giving your employees a forum to be heard by soliciting their input, is critical to eradicating employee disengagement. How do I know? I saw it in action firsthand through a major failure and a major success when I was responsible for the global Internal Communications department at Avaya. And both instances taught me valuable lessons.

You're Fired

My boss called me into her office to advise me that the company was about to lay off 5,000 employees. I quickly opened up my notebook and uncapped my pen, as I knew it would be my responsibility to write the communications plan outlining how we would communicate this news to the tens of thousands of global employees who would *not be terminated*.

> **ridiculous**
> [ree-di-kue-less]
> *adjective*
> 1. extremely silly or unreasonable.

I asked my boss the date that all employees would be notified and she said, "The CEO does not want to communicate this to all employees. He only wants to notify the employees who are impacted." I was shocked. How do you lay off thousands of global employees and not let everyone in the company know what's happening? My gut told me this was wrong, so I spoke up.

> But everyone is going to find out, I said.
> Employees will watch it on TV or read about it
> on the Internet. They'll also see their co-
> workers and friends in distress as they clean out
> their cubicles, and they'll realize that people who
> they work with in other functions have
> disappeared.

I was so passionate about this that I didn't stop pleading my case. Continuing,

We have to be open and honest. As soon as every impacted employee has been notified, we must communicate the news to the rest of the workforce; letting them know what's going on and why. We can't let this news spread organically on its own—we have to manage it. If we hide this news from employees it will destroy confidence in leadership and employee engagement. Employees will run in fear and become unproductive; they will hide in their foxholes ... afraid to move ... because they don't want to be the next person on the chopping block. The CEO must share this news with everyone and provide context, so the employees who are not terminated don't become disengaged.

THE TRUTH

If you hide news from employees it will destroy confidence in leadership and employee engagement.

This would be like putting your three kids to bed and the next morning, one kid has disappeared. No one talks about it—it's not allowed. Is this realistic? Of course not. The outcome is that a multitude of new problems are seeded from the get-go. I saw them coming as the tsunami began to build.

Something I said resonated with my boss—or it may have been the arm flailing that I threw in for dramatic effect. She responded, "I will go back to the CEO and let him know your thoughts."

A few days later my passionate plea was shot down. My boss informed me that the CEO did not agree and all employees would not be notified. I was heartbroken. I knew in my heart and my gut that the years of work we had done to successfully increase employee engagement were about to be flushed down the drain in one fell swoop, along with our enhanced reputation and soaring profitability. How right I was!

Impacted employees were notified around the globe and within hours you could hear a pin drop in Corporate Headquarters, a building that 3,000 people called home. For the next few weeks and months, the building was lifeless. There was limited energy and limited productivity, I received 80 percent fewer emails than usual, and the halls were empty.

THE TRUTH

When people are afraid of getting laid off, they run underground and hide in fear. They don't make a move or stick their head out of their foxhole because they think it's safer to hide and not be on anyone's radar.

As I suspected, employees ran underground and hid in fear. People were afraid to make a move or stick their head out of their foxhole, because they thought it was safer to hide and not be on anyone's radar. Employees were immobilized.

Remember those employee engagement strides that I spoke about in the first chapter? To jog your memory, we worked for two years to drive a six- to 16-point increase in three employee engagement survey categories and moved the overall Corporate Employee Engagement score from 51 to 62 percent. The year we made the decision to not be open and honest with employees about this mass layoff, our employee engagement scores plummeted 20 points. That decision wiped out more than two years' worth of blood, sweat, tears, and progress.

For months, the main topic of conversation among employees who had not been laid off was how disrespected they felt. While I know I cannot attribute all of the engagement loses to this event, I was there, and can tell you that not being transparent had a major impact on how employees felt about the work environment, company, and leadership team.

THE TRUTH

Share critical non-confidential information with your people in the moment, in an effort to keep them productive and engaged.

All the senior leaders had to do was communicate openly and honestly, and the outcome of this event would have been different. The employees who remained in the company may not have been happy, but they would have felt in-the-know and respected. Employees also would have had information about why that difficult decision was made and what business plans leaders had to avoid another mass layoff. I'm not talking about assuring people that it would not happen again, that's irresponsible to do. Instead, I'm talking about sharing critical non-confidential information with your people in the moment, in an effort to keep them productive and engaged.

You're Hired

One year later, the same leaders got a wake-up call. Avaya's stock price was down and private equity owners were circling. Avaya was going to be delisted from the New York Stock Exchange and converted from a publicly held company to a private company. Senior leaders knew that in order to get top dollar for the company, they needed to get their house in order.

In an effort to engage employees, I was asked to lead an eight-week initiative that enabled 18,000 global workers to gather in small groups of 10 to 15 people. Every employee participated in a cross-functional, interactive, facilitator-run 90-minute session. The small groups engaged in lively conversations about where the company has been, where the company is currently, and where the company is going. When the groups got to the part where they discussed the future of the company, the facilitator took notes about ideas employees had to improve the business.

THE TRUTH

In the face of being delisted from the New York Stock Exchange, employees were on a high because leaders asked for and listened to their input.

Employee ideas gathered in the 1,500 sessions were compiled by my global Internal Communications team and reviewed by the senior leadership team, who implemented many of the recommendations as they transformed the new private business. Then we did what all Champions would have done. We embarked on an internal communications campaign where we let employees know that their input is valued and what ideas we would act upon.

Needless to say, the reaction was extraordinary. More than 1,000 employees sent emails to the initiative's mailbox saying this was the most engaging and inspiring activity they have ever been involved in during their career. Many also praised the senior leadership team for being open to hearing their thoughts and ideas, and implementing employee's suggestions.

Here we were being delisted from the New York Stock Exchange, and employees were on a high because we asked for and listened to their input. They felt like they had a say in the company's new direction and it felt good. Asking your employees for their ideas—and truly listening to what they have to say—means more to them than any glass paper weight or water bottle imprinted with the company logo.

Avaya learned a painful lesson from the massive layoffs of the previous year. Because of finally listening to its remaining workforce and engaging them proactively in the change, it was able to climb out of the morale hole it had dug itself into. However, many of these leaders were ultimately replaced by leaders chosen by the new private equity owners.

Get Your Head in the Clouds

Jim Whitehurst, CEO at Red Hat, understands the power of collaboration and open management. Red Hat is the world's largest provider of open-source solutions, providing software to 90 percent of Fortune 500 companies. It is the inventor of the Linux operating system with a stated goal of becoming the single leader of enterprise cloud computing. At $5 billion in market cap, it's clear that Red Hat is doing a lot of things right, and employee engagement is one of them.

Red Hat leaders make the majority of their decisions and management procedures transparent to employees, using input from the workforce. It also gives every employee access to a global mailing list where anyone can post ideas and news. By opening up the decision-making process and giving employees an easy way to collaborate, the workforce is engaged and revenue is soaring. Red Hat's stock? It has doubled.

Now Get Your Head Out of the Clouds

Many leaders think if they don't share information with employees that no harm is done. However, you are a Champion, so I'm expecting more from you. Trust is established when leaders share both positive and negative news. Employees are smart. Many times they know when something is wrong and they also sense when leaders are not doing their "fair share" of information sharing. If you are a stingy communicator, employees will be disengaged and your bottom line will suffer. There's simply no good reason for it. There are many vehicles that you can use to communicate with employees on a regular basis. Find the ones that are most effective for both you and your employees; and use them!

Communicate openly and honestly. Use every opportunity, touchpoint, and channel at your disposal, and your employee engagement levels will take a path that is directionally correct—I promise.

WHAT A CHAMPION WOULD DO NEXT

- Partner with your Internal Communications organization or contact to conduct an audit and implement changes:
  - Do you have a robust plan where you use every opportunity, touchpoint, and channel at your disposal, to ensure employees are in the know?
  - Do you have two-way communication vehicles— avenues to gather feedback from employees—and a plan to share that feedback with leaders?
  - Are you thanking employees for their input and closing the loop, communicating which ideas will be implemented?
  - Do you have avenues for employees to communicate with one another?
- Add your Internal Communications leader to your Executive Leadership Team. This will ensure he/she is aware of everything that it going on in your company and can make recommendations about opportunities to communicate with employees.
- Commit to being more transparent, open, and honest. You are a Champion … you got this!

Get the right person in every chair, create a line of sight between what employees do day-to-day and the company's goals, and build a two-way communication culture, and you are three steps ahead.

CHAPTER 5

Recognize People

The deepest desire of the human spirit is to be acknowledged.

—Stephen Covey, Author, *7 Habits of Highly Effective People*

When I was young, my school designated a "Field Day" every spring. Students were entered into three events and you could win colorful ribbons that shouted out, "I'm the best!" The blue ribbon represented First Place, the yellow ribbon represented Second Place, and the red ribbon represented Third Place.

If you came in first, second, or third without cheating, the reward was a shiny ribbon that you ran around the field with or proudly taped or thumbtacked to the wall in your bedroom for all to see. On that particular Field Day, you rocked and it felt amazing.

Then one day, my 9-year-old world came crashing down. I was participating in my third Field Day event running wildly down the uneven dirt course. The egg that I was balancing on a metal spoon flipped off, and bright yellow yolk streamed through the spotty blades of green grass beneath my feet. For the first time ever on a Field Day, I didn't receive a ribbon in an event I participated in. I was crushed. I wasn't the winner—I wasn't the best.

Alone, I walked to the side of my elementary school, sat on the ground against the red brick wall, and cried. In that moment, for the first time ever, I felt what it was like to lose. Yes, I had lost at things in my life before, but losing a sport was entirely another thing. For me, losing a sporting event was not an option. I don't know if balancing an egg on a spoon qualifies as a sporting event, but my Texas elementary school seemed to think so.

THE TRUTH

To: Every kid who has ever been picked last for a team in school during mandatory Physical Education class
Message: I'm sorry.
From: A new wave of leaders

When I pulled myself together, I walked back to the field where the three winners were jumping up and down excitedly with their ribbons. It hurt and I felt left out. I felt like I had failed. I felt like I wasn't good enough. I felt sorry for every kid who had ever been picked last for a team in school during mandatory Physical Education class. It was an "aha" moment for me.

Why "Everybody's a Winner" Doesn't Work

Fast forward to today. In many public school systems, everybody's a winner on Field Day. Ribbons are awarded for first, second, and third place, and every student who did not "win" receives a ribbon even though they fell down in a pile of dirt while running the three-legged race or allowed their egg to shatter and spew yellow yolk into the green grass.

While the feeling that I had when I did not "ribbon" on Field Day hurt, I'm glad the "everybody's a winner" system didn't exist when I was in elementary school. Why? Because that system would have disengaged me. I would have been less motivated to work hard. I would have wondered why the bar was set so low. I would have been less inclined to be creative or to take a risk. I would have felt like my efforts were being devalued.

The reality is ... not everyone is a winner.

> **recognition**
> [rek-uhg-nish-uhn]
> *noun*
> 1. the acknowledgment of achievement
> conveying approval or sanction.

Paul L. Marciano, author of *Carrots and Sticks Don't Work*, says,

> Over the past several decades, organizations
> have spent billions of dollars creating and
> implementing reward and recognition

programs, in the hopes of motivating their employees and increasing morale. This approach seems to make good sense, however, in terms of return on investment, the numbers don't add up. Most programs intended to motivate employees actually create an overall deficit in employee motivation. While a handful of employees may be reinforced, many are left feeling punished.

Then Who Do I Recognize?

If you are no longer going to only reward your high performers with your version of blue, yellow, and red Field Day ribbons, and you are no longer going to give company-branded coffee mugs to the masses regardless of their results (the "everybody's a winner" approach), how do you recognize people in a way that drives employee engagement?

There's nothing more effective in the workplace—and in life in general—than a sincere thank you for a job well done. That's it. Be it written or spoken, the most powerful form of recognition in the world is to know that we matter and are appreciated ... it's one of the greatest human needs. The power of a thank you to the employee, and verbal recognition of his or her contribution to the rest of your team and throughout the company, cannot be understated.

THE TRUTH

Giving company-branded coffee mugs to the masses regardless of their results does not engage a workforce.

Many leaders think that the paycheck an employee receives each week or month is thanks enough. However, if this was true, the world wouldn't have an employee disengagement crisis on its hands, would it?

Doug Conant gets it. Conant is the former CEO of Campbell's and co-author of *TouchPoints: Creating Powerful Leadership Connections in the Smallest of Moments*. When he joined the global food giant, it was experiencing a significant decline in market value. Conant transformed the global leadership team (clearly, he understood the importance of getting the right person in every chair), reconfigured the portfolio, cut costs, and made strategic investments. His mission to achieve superior employee engagement levels was also a crucial contributor to the company's turnaround. For the 10 years that he led Campbell's, Conant wrote 10 to 20 handwritten thank you notes every day, six days a week. That's 30,000 thank you notes a year.

Under Conant's leadership, employee engagement at Campbell Soup went from being among the worst in the Fortune 500 to being consistently among the best. If you think this achievement yielded shareholder returns in the top tier of the global food industry, you are correct.

Returns for All

Another added benefit to verbal recognition is that it's a two-way street. The employee on the receiving end of the thank you benefits and you do too.

Recent studies published in the *Journal of Personality and Social Psychology* tell us, "Being grateful can improve well-being, physical health, strengthen social relationships, produce positive emotional states, and help us cope with stressful times in our lives. We say thank you because we want the other person to know we value what they've done for us and, maybe, encourage them to help us again in the future."

Those who were thanked were more willing to provide further assistance. Indeed the effect of 'thank you' was quite substantial. While only 32 percent of participants who received a neutral email volunteered to help again, when the leader expressed his gratitude, volunteerism skyrocketed to 66 percent.

THE TRUTH

There's nothing more effective in the workplace—and in your personal life—than a sincere thank you for a job well done. That's it.

Sincere-Timely-Specific: The Golden Ticket

The key to rewarding people well is that the recognition must be sincere, timely, and specific. Sending an email that says "Great job" to an entire team a week after a major product launch is not going to cut it. Face-to-face recognition, a phone call, or a hand-written note is much more effective than sending an email.

- **Be Sincere:** The most important part of saying thank you is being sincere. People are smart. If you thank them out of obligation, they'll know. Speak confidently, showing that you mean every word you say, and be honest. Open up and speak from your heart.

- **Be Timely:** It's more effective to dole out the praise as close to the timing of the event as possible vs. waiting days or weeks to thank the employee. When an employee is thanked in real-time, it reinforces the positive behaviors that the employee exhibited.

- **Be Specific:** When recognizing an employee, content is king. The recognition must be specific to the person and highlight his/her role in the accomplishment. When people are praised for something specific, it increases the likelihood that they will repeat the positive behavior.

Finally, recognition pays dividends for months to come. Margie Warrell, author of *Stop Playing Safe*, says,

> Actively supporting people to be more successful puts deposits into the relationships bank account that can make a crucial difference when circumstances change and the chips are down. Studies have found that how we support and celebrate people when they are enjoying success makes an even bigger impact on our relationships with them than how we support them in times of crisis.

Don't underestimate the power of a simple thank you, Champ. Be it written or spoken, the most powerful form of recognition in the world is to know that we matter and are appreciated. Recognition is one of the greatest human needs. Therefore, when it occurs on a regular basis it will help create an environment that people love where they can soar, so your company meets or exceeds its goals. Saying "thank you" often is a simple and inexpensive way to fuel your employees—and your employee engagement levels—forward. I know you get it because you are a Champion. Thank you for being you.

WHAT A CHAMPION WOULD DO NEXT

- Buy a box of thank you cards. Make that 50 boxes.
- As the last thig you do each workday, write and distribute 10 handwritten thank you notes that are sincere, timely and specific. In fact, you can set-up a standing meeting notice for yourself at 5 p.m. each day to accomplish this critical task.
- Add "Recognition" as a component to your staff meeting and to any large group meeting that you lead, and celebrate the wins.
- Ask your team members to speak up at your staff meeting, thanking anyone who went above and beyond the call of duty.
- Partner with your Human Resources department or person to audit your company's current recognition program. If you have a traditional program in place, replace it with a "thank you for a job well done" program that enables both people managers and employees to recognize one another.
- Share these ideas with all people managers and ask them to follow suit.
- Smile. Your efforts are improving employee engagement.

Get the right person in every chair, create a line of sight between what employees do day-to-day and the company's goals, create a two-way communication culture, and recognize people, and you are half-way to turning around your employee disengagement crisis.

PART TWO
Four Ways You Need to Be

CHAPTER 6
Be Self-Confident

Your time is limited, so don't waste it living someone else's life. Don't be trapped by dogma—which is living with the results of other people's thinking. Don't let the noise of others' opinions drown out your own inner voice. And most important, have the courage to follow your heart and intuition.

—Steve Jobs, Apple Visionary

If I had a magic wand and could give everyone in the world one gift, it would be self-confidence. We've been programmed to believe that we are ordinary or not enough, yet the truth is that we are amazing, magnificent, powerful beings. Because of this negative conditioning, however, we unconsciously live in fear.

Danger, Will Robinson, Danger
I choose to live a different way. I believe that much of the danger we dream up is not real, but in our minds. I believe irrational fear is one of the greatest barriers to success. It does not keep you safe, my friends, irrational fear immobilizes you.

fear
[fir]
verb
1. to expect or worry about something bad
or unpleasant.

Rational fears, such as the fear of being bitten by a rattlesnake that is slithering toward you on a dirt path, are legitimate and exist to prevent bad things from happening. However, much of the fear we experience is irrational. It's not real; *fear is the story we tell ourselves thanks to our negative conditioning.* Then, when we hear the voice of fear in our head, we panic, we freeze, we become average, even below average. We stop shooting for the stars and start shooting for mediocrity—why? Because we think being mediocre is safe. Champions know that this is a lie.

So what should you do when you hear the voice of irrational fear in your head? TC North, PhD, a high-performance executive coach, says that if you run from irrational fear you will feed it, so you must be courageous and face it head on. To avoid going down the disastrous rabbit hole of irrational fear, follow these steps:

1. Identify the fear.
2. Acknowledge and embrace the fear.
3. Dis-identify with the fear. You are not your fears.
4. Define the worst-case scenario.

5. Do a reality check. How probable is it that the worst-case scenario will happen (0-100 percent). Exactly—the probability is very low.

6. Refocus. Create a fearless focus on what you want, imagine being in control and see your success.

In addition to relegating us to being average or even below average, fear negatively impacts our decision-making process. When a person fears rejection, which is one of the four biggest fears, he/she will do whatever is necessary to fit in and be accepted; even if the decision carries with it negative consequences. The need for validation, belonging, and acceptance over-rides our logical brain and gut feeling. This phenomenon is also known as "peer pressure."

Peers are an important influence on our behavior and peer pressure is a rite of passage for most adolescents. However, the result is usually bad, as it leads to acts involving delinquency, drug or alcohol abuse, sexual promiscuity, and reckless driving. Think back to a time when you didn't want to be rejected, so you went along with the crowd. My guess is the experience is not listed on your resume or CV as one of your finer moments. I know my "peer pressure" moments aren't. Be self-confident; face fear head on.

Conformity Sucks

When I was young, I jumped for joy whenever I was given a new box of Crayola crayons and a coloring book.

The bigger the box of crayons, the more excited I was, as it meant more opportunities to create a colorful masterpiece. I also remember my excitement as I ran to my mother after finishing a page in the book to show her my Picasso. "That's beautiful," she would say. "You did a great job coloring within the lines."

THE TRUTH

It's the people who color outside of the lines who make magic—the inventors, the innovators, the pioneers, and the non-conformers.

In that moment, Mom was attempting to program me. I was praised for coloring inside the lines if I followed "her instructions," something that my gut said not to do. As adults, we get that it's the people who color outside of the lines who make magic. The inventors, the innovators, the pioneers, the non-conformers—these are the people who make things happen in this world.

Yet most of us are discouraged from being different and coloring outside of the lines. Even more are discouraged from eliminating the lines. In many cases this means we're discouraged from being ourselves. I don't fault my mom for this. She was an incredibly uplifting, positive person, who was also praised as a child for coloring inside the lines by my grandmother. It's all they knew and they were doing their best.

TRUTH

You were not created to conform. You exist to be uniquely you and to make a difference in the world.

You were not created to conform. *You* exist to be uniquely you and to make a difference in the world. *You* will not have completed your journey until you put your piece of the puzzle in place, which takes self-confidence and a belief in yourself.

We come into this world as assets, not liabilities. However, our thinking changes with our environment and our conditioning. Too many times, the messages we hear are negative, ending dreams, and driving thoughts and behaviors that do not support the building of Champions.

They Meant Well, But They Lied

Where are you on your journey to becoming more self-confident? If you still have work to do, a good place to begin is by seeing the truth: much of what you have been told in your life is a lie. You are not stupid, wrong, worthless, or a disappointment. You are an amazing, magnificent, and powerful being, and you hold an incredibly important piece of the puzzle in your hands.

The world will not be complete without you and your specific contribution. Yes, you Champ.

You also begin by not seeking the acceptance of people around you. When you accept yourself as is, development areas and all, you'll gain self-confidence and the opinions of others won't matter. Besides, you don't need other people to validate you or your thoughts and ideas, because the answers are already inside of you. All you have to do is trust your gut instinct.

THE TRUTH

Your gut is an incredible tool—a powerful internal radar system. Use it.

Intuition is "knowing" something without being able to explain how you came to that conclusion rationally. It's that "gut feeling" or "instinct" that research says is right 95 percent of the time. It means depending on something that you don't understand and it's how you tap into your subconscious mind, which is where you "archive" all kinds of information that you don't remember on a conscious level.

Your gut is an incredible tool—a powerful internal radar system. Use it and stop being concerned about how you look in the eyes of others, what they think, and whether they approve of you. *You can only control you.*

Not Taking Vacation Days Sucks

Speaking of not being concerned about how you look in the eyes of others, when is the last time you used all of your allotted vacation days and encouraged your team members to do the same?

According to internal research by audit firm EY (formerly Ernst & Young), employees who use more vacation days are rated higher, have less stress, have lower turnover rates, have improved mental skills, and increased productivity.

Most employees ignore this advice. Unused vacation days are at a 40-year high. According to a study by Oxford Economics, U.S. workers are using only 77 percent of their paid time off. In total, that's about 169 million days forfeited, amounting to $52.4 billion in lost benefits.

John de Graaf, executive director of the nonprofit Take Back Your Time, says, "There are many reasons why Americans don't take all their vacation time. A lot of people are fearful of the workload they'll come back to and feel they have to work longer to keep up with the pace of their co-workers."

THE TRUTH

If you really believed in yourself, you'd take every vacation day you've earned.

Fear and lack of self-confidence will do you in every time. If you really believed in yourself, Champ, you'd take every vacation day you've earned. If you have the right person in every chair, surely you have people on your team who you can delegate work to in your absence, so you do not return to an enormous workload.

If you think that you couldn't possibly burden your staff that way; think again. When my Vice President put me in charge when she was on vacation; I was elated. I had been entrusted with the organization in her absence. It was a vote of confidence.

Motivational speaker Les Brown got it right when he said, "Too many of us are not living our dreams because we are living our fears." Please don't be one of those people. Taking time off to recharge is a no brainer. Act like the Champion you are and do it ... please.

What Confidence Looks Like in Action

One day I went into my boss' office and presented a plan for a major global project. She asked, "Where's your plan B?"

"I don't have a Plan B. If I didn't think Plan A is going to work, it wouldn't be my Plan A."

Clearly, she wasn't prepared for my response. She then asked, "What if it fails?"

"It's not going to fail. When we roll out Plan A, we will have our finger on the pulse of how things are going and will make course corrections. I've done my homework and am confident that the crux of my plan is spot on."

That didn't stop her as she said, "I don't think it's a good idea to not have a back-up plan for something this big."

Matching her with strength in my voice, I replied, "If it completely fails, you can fire me. I'm confident that this is going to be a success, so I don't think it's a good use of my time or talents to develop plans B and C."

Looking at me, she said nothing in return. I then proceeded to lead a global team who rolled out the solo Plan A.

The result? It was one of the most successful initiatives the company has ever seen, requiring minor course corrections. You may be thinking that you could never do such a thing, but I beg to differ. This is what self-confidence looks like. It's strong. It's unwavering. It's empowering. It will enable you and your team to cross the finish line first the majority of the time.

 THE TRUTH

Most people condition others to fail.
Don't buy into mediocrity and the lies.
Champions can accomplish anything they
set their minds to.

You see, most people are still programming you—and me—to fail. However, we must refuse to buy into mediocrity and the lies. Champions know that they, and their team, can accomplish anything they set their minds to. Failure is not an option! Tentative leaders make for tentative employees. If you're confident, your people will be as well, and you will be in a great position to lead an employee engagement revolution.

WHAT A CHAMPION WOULD DO NEXT

- Read this every morning: Much of what I have been told in my life is a lie. I am an amazing, magnificent, and powerful being. I hold an incredibly important piece of the puzzle in my hands. The world will not be complete without me and my specific contribution. I'm a Champion!
- Stop seeking the acceptance of people around you. Accept yourself as is—development areas and all—and the opinions of others won't matter.
- Follow your gut.
- Schedule a vacation to a magnificent destination and encourage your team members to do the same.
- Pat yourself on the back for growing and having more self-confidence.
- Send me a postcard … please.

Get the right person in every chair, create a line of sight between what employees do day-to-day and the company's goals, build a two-way communication culture, recognize people, and be confident, and you are five steps ahead.

CHAPTER 7

Be Courageous

Follow the path of the unsafe, independent thinker. Expose your ideas to the danger of controversy. Speak your mind and fear less the label of 'crackpot' than the stigma of conformity.

— Thomas J. Watson, IBM Founder

Your life is your choice. Are you going to play big or play small? Are you going to be shackled by fear or have confidence in yourself and live courageously? Unfortunately, most people choose the former. This explains why 90 percent of people in this world are in the middle or below average performance categories. They never realize their full potential by putting their piece of the puzzle in place.

Fear is a debilitating emotion. As I mentioned in the previous chapter, irrational fear does not keep you safe, it immobilizes you. It paralyzes you into inaction, which changes the course of your life and the lives of the seven billion other people who you share the planet with. Yes, irrational fear is that impactful! When you choose not to act and fulfill your destiny, you rob yourself and world of your gift—a gift that only you have been given.

So what's the alternative? To live courageously ... to live like the Champion you are. Winnie the Pooh had it right when he said, "Always remember you are braver than you believe, smarter than you seem, and stronger than you think!" Yes, bears talk. Maybe you should listen.

Courageous Act No. 1 — Speak Up

In addition to being conditioned to fail, most of us have been conditioned to remain silent; to believe that our voice does not matter. Stop believing the lies. The same way that there's a cost by not putting your piece of the puzzle in place in this world, there's a cost of not speaking up, and it is usually significant.

THE TRUTH

Your life is your choice. Are you going to play big or play small? Are you going to be shackled by fear, or have confidence in yourself and live courageously?

People come into this world as assets, not as liabilities, but our environment and our negative conditioning drives our thoughts and behaviors. When I was young, I was regularly told to stop talking in class, so other people could "have their turn." All I can say now is: thank goodness I came out of the womb somehow knowing that I was being fed a series of lies. If

I had not, I would have silenced my voice, hiding the "real" me from the world. Looking back, what kind of encouragement is that for someone to ask more questions, voice their thoughts, color outside the lines, and think the impossible? It teaches people to stay quiet, to conform, to be mediocre.

> **courage**
> [kur-ij]
> *noun*
> 1. the quality of mind or spirit that enables
> a person to face difficulty, danger, or pain
> without fear; bravery.

If you are thinking something and not saying it, there are 10 other people in the room thinking the same and choosing the safe route ... silence. Why? Because they are afraid and they assume someone else will speak up. If you want to be a leader who is respected, admired, and appreciated by others, tactfully speak up and tell it like it is. This is how Champions act.

Courageous Act No. 2 — Lead with Your Heart
Another key element of courage is leading with your heart. Companies today are riddled by those running them with their head and not enough people running businesses with their heart.

THE TRUTH

> We're told that bringing your heart or emotions into the workplace is weak and soft, and we listened. It's a lie that encourages us to not be ourselves.

No wonder—the world teaches us limitation and has told us lies since we were young children, silencing our passion and emotions.

One of the biggest lies we've been told is to leave your heart at the door. We're told that bringing your heart or emotions into the workplace is weak and soft, and we listened. We believed it—only the "weak" expose who they really are. The outcome of that lie? It encourages us to go to work each and every day a shell of who we are. It's a lie that encourages us to not be ourselves. Thankfully, it's a lie that has been proven wrong.

There's a rash of new data that suggests while cognitive intelligence matters, emotional intelligence is just as important, or more so. You cannot drive human behavior and inspire an employee to reach for the stars when your feelings and emotions are absent. It's impossible.

THE TRUTH

You cannot drive human behavior and inspire an employee to reach for the stars when your feelings and emotions are absent. It's impossible.

A Towers Watson study illustrated that the greatest driver of employee engagement *worldwide* is whether people *feel* their managers and organizations have genuine concern for their well-being. Not think, but *feel*—with their heart.

One company that understands the importance of leading with the heart is Starbucks. In Joseph A. Michelli's book, *The Starbucks Experience*, Michelli reveals Starbucks' secret sauce according to a former Starbucks partner and consultant. "Starbucks is a human company—that's the difference. The biggest story about Starbucks is that it's as much about people as it is about the coffee."

Michelli goes on to say that the respect leadership offers employees is often reflected in the way in which employees respect and create an experience for one another. John Moore, a former partner with Starbucks notes, "What I truly found special about the store experience is that it is basically a family. What leadership offered to us, we offered to one another."

THE TRUTH

> Starbucks is a human company. It is successful because it's as much about people as it is about the coffee.

Leaders must act human ... bringing both their heart and their head to work ... encouraging their employees to do the same for both their co-workers and customers.

While every interaction that every customer has with Starbucks might not be flawless, from my experience, most Starbucks locations are more uplifting than other consumer products stores. Their employees appear to be happy and warm, produce few product errors, and are incredibly customer focused. Hmm, sounds like Starbucks is getting the right person in every chair and showing employees that what they do every day contributes to the company's success.

THE TRUTH

Your customers will never love your company until your employees love it first. And your employees can't fall in love with your company if they are conditioned to leave their heart at the door.

Finally, leading with your heart enables you to truly connect with your most important asset: your employees. Champ, if you think your most important asset is your customers, I respectfully disagree. Why? Because your customers will never love your company until your employees love it first. And your employees can't fall in love with your company if they are conditioned to leave their heart at the door.

Leading an employee engagement revolution takes courage. You can strengthen your "courage muscle" by speaking up and bringing your heart to work. These are two things that many people don't do; Champions do, however. Thanks, in advance, for stepping up. I knew you had it in you!

WHAT A CHAMPION WOULD DO NEXT

- Your life is a choice. Choose—right now—to start playing big.
- Speak up. Your voice matters and you have important things to contribute to this world. Everyone's voice matters.
- Bring your whole self to work with you ... head, heart, and all. It's not weak and soft; it's what Champions do.
- Remember, you are braver than you believe, smarter than you seem, and stronger than you think! Bears do talk and they get angry if you don't listen.

Get the right person in every chair, create a line of sight between what employees do day-to-day and the company's goals, build a two-way communication culture, recognize people, be confident and courageous, and you are six steps ahead.

CHAPTER 8

Be Present

The ability to be in the present moment is a major component of mental wellness.

—Abraham Maslow, Founder of Humanistic Psychology

A major driver of employee engagement is whether or not people feel their leaders have genuine concern for their well-being. The best way to do that is to engage in face-to-face communications with your people, all the while staying present and completely in the moment.

In some organizations, face-to-face has become almost non-existent. Yes, it is difficult to do in our tech-laden world where we are constantly inundated with messages and live in communication overload. We are bombarded with messages via Email, Pinterest, Facebook, Twitter, LinkedIn, Friendster, Instagram, Google+, Flickr, YouTube, Periscope, Blabs, Blogs, TV, Radio, Billboards, Online Banner Ads, Voice Mail, and Text, and are expected to respond virtually instantly. This takes us out of the moment and takes our focus away from what really matters: your employees and their engagement or lack thereof.

I say let's bring the dinosaur back.

THE TRUTH

By choosing to put down your electronic devices and be present, you will begin to realize some balance in your life.

In our society today, many people choose to be tied to their electronic devices 24/7. It's not uncommon to see a family of four at a restaurant eating dinner, all the while pecking away at their smartphones as if they were alone at the table. It is also not uncommon to receive a work email at 3 a.m. Even sadder, to see a person on a beach vacation surrounded by family and participating in a conference call.

Did You Say Carassius Auratus?

To add insult to injury, we're more distracted than ever. As reported in *Time* magazine, "The average attention span for the notoriously ill-focused goldfish is nine seconds." Also, according to a study from Microsoft Corp., "People now generally lose concentration after eight seconds, highlighting the effects of an increasingly digitalized lifestyle on the brain."

goldfish
[gohld-fish]
noun
1. a small, usually yellow or orange fish, Carassius Auratus, of the carp family,

native to China, bred in many varieties and
often kept in fishbowls and pools.

Is this really the dream you envisioned for your life as a child? To be less present than a bright orange fish that dwells in a bowl of water? I didn't think so, but this is our reality in our frenetic world, Champ. However, you can change it. One of the most magical gifts you can give anyone is to be fully present in the moment, as the human need to connect is still alive and well. Champions get this.

How To Be More Present than a Goldfish

Being in the moment enables you to be aware of everything that is happening around you. You are not thinking about what you are going to have for dinner or the soccer game you watched on TV yesterday. You are simply aware and all of your attention is focused on the moment at hand.

Here are a few ideas to help you on your journey to be more present than a goldfish:

- Turn off your phone during every meal and while you are asleep.
- Boycott Facebook for 30 days once a quarter.
- Check your personal email once a day.
- Leave your phone at home when you go outside to exercise.
- Boycott work while on vacation.
- Turn off your phone when interacting face-to-face with your employees.

Yes, You Really Can

If you are thinking that business people can't possibly live this way, NEWSFLASH: They can and they do! It's how I live ... by choice. You can choose it too. I'm proud to say that I have taken every vacation day ever allocated to me in my life, I do not work while on vacation, I regularly turn off my phone, and I've ended relationships with people because they choose to engage with their electronic device virtually 24/7.

Think about the last time you were with someone and they couldn't stop looking at their smartphone. How did you feel? Ignored or disengaged, I suspect. If you didn't feel disengaged, then you were also not being present in the moment. When you are in another person's presence, you owe it to that individual to give them your undivided attention and vice versa.

THE TRUTH

In business, everyone is a number, and anyone can get laid off for anything at any time.

If you are thinking that you are too important or too high up on the food chain at work to live this way, NEWSFLASH: you are not. In business, everyone is a number. I'm sorry to break that to you, but it's the truth. The fastest way to reduce expenses is to reduce people and all of the costs that come along with them. Even the CEO is just a number. Anyone can get laid off for anything at any time. I've seen it happen countless times in my journey through Corporate America and I was on the receiving end of a layoff the same year I was rated a high performer.

Yes, it takes self-confidence and courage to live in the moment, but you already possess these traits because you are a Champion. You read the previous chapters and took the words to heart. By choosing to put down your electronic device, you will begin to realize some balance in your life. You will ensure that you are in the moment, able to give your full attention to the people in your presence. This is a necessary component in order for you to know thy staff.

Know Thy Staff

By being present and in the moment, and by spending quality time getting to know your team, you'll demonstrate that you have genuine concern for their well-being. This is a major driver of employee engagement. Strong relationships will form and you'll also gain their trust—another key component in employee engagement. As reported by the global survey research and consulting organization, the National Research Business Institute, Inc.:

- 87 percent of engaged employees trust their manager.
- 57 percent of disengaged employees trust their manager.

In virtually every company I've consulted for, we conducted employee focus groups to determine what communication vehicle employees prefer to receive important news. The options included:

- Email
- Employee Publication (electronic or hard copy)
- Employee Intranet
- Video or Webinar
- Face-to-Face Large Team or Town Hall Meeting
- Face-to-Face Small Team Meeting or One-on-One Conversation
- Bulletin Board
- Social Media
- Grapevine or Watercooler Talk

In every company, which spanned seven industries, 70 percent of employees selected face-to-face small team meeting or one-on-one conversation as their preferred communications vehicle. So although we have many electronic communications vehicles at our fingertips, people still prefer human interaction. The need for us to "connect" with another human being is alive and well, and there's a person among us who has it mastered.

Bill Clinton's Cheat Sheet

Regardless of your political affiliation and stance on politics, Bill Clinton is a masterful relationship builder. John Corcoran, an aide in the Clinton White House, authored a whitepaper entitled *The Bill Clinton Method*

Cheat Sheet.   The paper documents Corcoran's observations about how President Clinton used several tactics to build relationships with people who cleaned the White House to people who were Heads of State:

- *Give every person your presence and undivided attention.* Tune everything else out, stand up straight, make eye contact, and take an interest in the person in front of you, making them feel like they are the ONLY person in the room.

- *Listen.* Really hear what the person is saying vs. figuring out how you are going to respond. Also, follow through on your conversation, even if it's something small like sending an article, as you'll demonstrate you were paying attention.

- *Keep it personal.* People enjoy talking about their personal passions and interests. When interacting with employees, have a human conversation by asking about a person's family, vacation plans, or hobbies.

- *Take a long-term view.* Slow and steady wins the race. Build relationships for the long term and you will always have people in your corner even in the darkest times.

Leaders must be present and fully in the moment, and know thy people. The more you get to know your people, the more they'll respect you. The more they respect you, the more engaged they'll be. The more engaged they are, the smarter they'll work.

Act like the Champion you are. Put down your electronic device and give every person in your presence your undivided attention. This modification will skyrocket the level of trust employees have in you and your company's employee engagement score.

WHAT A CHAMPION WOULD DO NEXT

- Choose to stop being tied to your electronic device. Yes, it's a choice.
- Implement several of the ideas to help you on your journey to be more present than a goldfish.
- Go do something fun with the free time that you now have on your hands.
- Ramp up face-to-face communications with your employees and when interacting with people:
  - Give your undivided attention.
  - Listen—really hear what the person is saying.
  - Ask about a person's family, vacation plans, or hobbies.
  - Build relationships for the long term.
- Congratulate yourself for triumphing over a Carassius Auratus. Goldfish have nothing on you.

Get the right person in every chair, create a line of sight between what employees do day-to-day and the company's goals, build a two-way communication culture, recognize people, be confident, courageous and present, and you are seven steps ahead.

CHAPTER 9

Be Optimistic

Perpetual optimism is a force multiplier.
— General Colin Powell, Former U.S. Secretary of State

T. Harv Eker knows a thing or two about the power of being optimistic, and it's key to his success and many of those who followed his words. In his #1 NY Times best-selling book, *Secrets of the Millionaire Mind*, Eker reveals the missing link between wanting success and achieving success: "The fact is that your character, thinking, and beliefs are a critical part of what determines the level of your success."

The Choice is Up to You
Eker adds:

> No thought lives in your head rent-free. Every thought you have will be an investment or a cost. It will either move you toward happiness and success or away from it. It will either empower you or disempower you. That's why it is

imperative you choose your thoughts and beliefs wisely.

I couldn't have said it better myself. For the most part, everything in your life is a choice—you were born with *free will*. How your life turns out will be a direct reflection of the choices you make while you are alive.

THE TRUTH

No thought lives in your head rent-free. Every thought you have will be an investment or a cost. It will either move you toward happiness and success or away from it. It will either empower you or disempower you.

Yes, some things happen to us that we do not choose, but when you take your last breath, what you experienced on Earth will largely be due to the choices you made and the choices you didn't make. Champions know this.

optimism
[op-tee-miz-um]
noun
1. a feeling or belief that good things will happen in the future.

Being upbeat, positive, and optimistic is a choice. Your thoughts are also a choice. You can choose to be empowered or disempowered, positive or negative—to be a gift or a cancer to the world. You have it within your own power to self-generate positivity whenever you choose.

When Bad Things Happen to Good People

Dr. Dennis Charney is the dean of Mount Sinai School of Medicine. He has examined more than 700 Vietnam War veterans who were held for more than five years as prisoners of war (POWs). Even though the men endured torture and solitary confinement, they did not develop depression or post-traumatic stress disorder once released. Why?

Once out of captivity, Charney interviewed the men and identified 10 characteristics that enabled them to emerge from the experience in better condition than most POWs. The number one characteristic was optimism, followed by altruism: the unselfish regard for or the devotion to the welfare of others. Humor and having a meaning in life (think placing your piece in the puzzle) also ranked high on the captive's list.

Countless other studies have been conducted on optimism, and the vast majority of them point to the vast benefits of being a positive person. Maybe most importantly, being optimistic is healthy. Optimists have better functioning immune systems, are less prone to addictions, cope better with difficult circumstances, and live longer. By thinking optimistically, you can increase your odds of living longer. A recent study at the Mayo

Clinic found that pessimism is a risk factor for premature death, even when other risk factors such as age and sex are discarded.

I'd Like an O, Please

What's the difference between an optimist and a pessimist? When a pessimist loses a sports competition in life, he/she will think, "I'm a failure and I can't do anything right." When an optimist loses a sports competition, he/she will think, "I must have not played my best today, but I know I'll play better next time!"

THE TRUTH

Optimists have better functioning immune systems, are less prone to addictions, cope better with difficult circumstances, and live longer.

When an event happens to a person, he/she views it as either positive or negative:

- Did it happen because of me (internal) or something or someone else (external)?
- Will this always happen to me (unchangeable) or can I change what caused it (changeable)?
- Is this something that affects all aspects of my life (pervasive) or was it a solitary occurrence (limited)?

Pessimistic people tend to view problems as internal, unchangeable, and pervasive, whereas optimistic people tend to take the most hopeful view of events and expect a favorable outcome.

No One Likes a Debbie Downer, Except on TV

While we all know people who are negative, one of the most popular fictional characters of our time is Debbie Downer. This character debuted on *Saturday Night Live* in 2004 and is still incredibly popular today. Wikipedia refers to Debby Downer as, "Someone who frequently adds bad news and negative feelings to a gathering, thus bringing down the mood of everyone around them." That sounds like crap, doesn't it, Champ?

I can assure you that as a leader, if you "frequently add bad news and negative feelings to a gathering, thus bringing down the mood of everyone around you," your team's employee engagement survey scores will be negative, just like your attitude. People have no desire to work with someone who drags them down when they can surround themselves with people who lift them up. People want to surround themselves with Champions.

THE TRUTH

Half of the world's population lives on less than $2.50 USD per day. Does your salary seem low now?

In life, you will experience ups and downs, but I challenge you to put things in perspective. If you are reading this book, odds are pretty good that you have a job, benefits, make enough money to live comfortably, and can even afford to go out to dinner this month. Compare that with the three-and-a-half billion people in this world—half of our population—who live on less than $2.50 USD per day. Does your salary seem low now?

I was recently at a meeting where a man shared that he was working in the World Trade Center in New York City on Sept. 11, 2011. On this day, the Islamic group called al-Qaeda coordinated a series of terrorist attacks in the United States, killing 3,000 people. His body was pulled out of the rubble at the base of the second tower. A lightbulb went off in my head when he said, "I thought I had bad days at work before, but when this happened to me I realized I hadn't. I've never had a bad day at work since."

You see, it's all about your perspective. Each day, your brain will generate 50,000 thoughts. Every thought will have an investment or a cost attached to it. Every thought will either move you toward happiness and success, or away from it. Every thought will either empower you or disempower you. Champions choose their thoughts wisely and quickly discard thoughts that don't help them rise up.

Find the Chuck in You

While it's unrealistic to be upbeat all the time, after all, there are things in life that will hurt you, your goal should be to deal with the rough spots and move on as quickly as possible. In addition, what if, starting right now, you stopped viewing your rough spots as a setback, and started viewing them as a setup for something better to happen?

What if, right now you choose to be as optimistic as Chuck in Castaway? This wildly popular movie stars Oscar ® winner Tom Hanks as a FedEx employee stranded on an uninhabited island after his plane crashes in the South Pacific. Chuck is saved by an inflatable life-raft, but loses the raft's emergency locator transmitter. Once washed up on an island, he discovers that it is uninhabited.

From having to bury a pilot's corpse to failing at every escape attempt, Chuck gets visibly weaker and thinner, but he never gives up hope. In an effort to stay strong, he draws a face with his bloody hand on a volleyball, names it Wilson, and begins talking to it. Four years later, Chuck makes his most admirable escape attempt yet, but his makeshift raft is battered by a storm, launching Wilson into the ocean, leaving Chuck overwhelmed by loneliness and sadness at the loss of his "friend and companion" Wilson. Eventually, a passing cargo ship finds Chuck drifting, and saves his life.

Why is this movie so popular? Because every moviegoer roots for Chuck and sees a piece of themself in him. No one thinks Chuck is crazy for drawing a face with his bloody hand on a volleyball, naming it Wilson, and talking to it. We all think it is magical that he displayed amazing courage and stayed optimistic even though he lived alone for four long years on a deserted island, enduring multiple challenges and setbacks. Yet with each, he took another step forward.

THE TRUTH

As a leader, you are a role model. People are watching you. Choose to focus on the positive rather than the negative and it will go a long way toward creating an environment that people love.

As a leader, you are a role model—a Champion. People are watching you. Choose to focus on the positive rather than the negative. Choose happiness rather than misery. Choose to be a beacon of light rather than a black cloud. Choose to believe that you will crack the code of employee disengagement in your company and create an environment that people love. Your optimism will make you feel more engaged and will go a long way toward re-engaging your workforce. I promise!

WHAT A CHAMPION WOULD DO NEXT

- Buy a volleyball.
- Draw a face on it.
- Name it.
- Place it in your office.
- Look at the volleyball whenever you are thinking negative thoughts, and have gratitude that you are not a castaway.
- Think back on your life and realize there has never been a storm that didn't pass. Storms make landfall and then break apart … *always*.
- Go forth and choose positive thoughts, lifting yourself and others up.
- Say "thank you" to the volleyball every now and then. It, too, needs to know that he matters and is appreciated. Just do it with your door closed.

Get the right person in every chair, create a line of sight between what employees do day-to-day and the company's goals, build a two-way communication culture, recognize people, be confident, courageous, present and optimistic, and you will have an engaged workforce on your hands.

CHAPTER 10

Tag, You're It

I've missed more than 9,000 shots in my career. I've lost almost 300 games. Twenty-six times, I've been trusted to take the game winning shot and missed. I've failed over and over and over again in my life. And that is why I succeed.

—— Michael Jordan, Basketball Player, Businessman, Olympian

If you step up and "own" this issue, you will move mountains and crack the code of employee disengagement in your company. Take the winning shot. If you miss, shoot again. And again. And again. *If not you, who?*

> **champion**
> [cham-pee-uhn]
> *noun*
> 1. you.

No One Can Bench You, But You

At times in my career I failed, but I never stayed on the bench for long. I believed in myself, and mustered the confidence, courage, presence, and optimism to keep forging ahead. I also spoke up a lot and walked through my building's entrance every day wearing my heart on my sleeve.

Eventually, I was rewarded. I was part of a leadership team in a large, global, complex, political organization. Together, using the concepts in this book, we cracked the code of employee disengagement. If we could succeed in that environment, you can succeed in yours.

Employee engagement does not have to be difficult. People simply want to know they are making a difference, know their voice is being heard, and know they are appreciated.

Here's your game plan:

WHAT YOU ARE GOING TO DO NEXT, CHAMPION

Step 1: Choose to Become "Who You Need To Be"

How your life turns out will be a direct reflection of the choices you make while you are alive. Step-up and choose to live big. I mean really, are you ever excited when you order the small ice cream cone?

- Be Confident
- Be Courageous
- Be Present
- Be Optimistic

Step 2: Gather Baseline Employee Engagement Data

You must know your employee engagement starting point, so you can measure your progress. Keep the survey short. Companies often use surveys that are hundreds of questions long, making it difficult for leaders to act on all of low-scoring questions or sections. If you pose a question on the survey, you must be prepared to address the area if it scores low. Therefore, only ask about specific areas where you are in a position to act and make changes.

Step 3: Choose to Do "What You Need To Do"

I could have developed multiple employee engagement solutions for different geographical regions and ages and sexes and tenures, and blah, blah, blah. However, I didn't do that. Why? Because it's not that complicated. Do these four things and you'll get measurable results.

- Get the Right Person in Every Chair
- Create a Line of Sight Between What Employees Do Day-to-Day and the Company's Goals
- Build a Two-Way Communication Culture

- Recognize People

Step 4: Gather Data and Make Modifications Based on Feedback

The lowest scoring statement on most employee engagement surveys is, "I trust leaders will act on my feedback." Don't be that leader.

Take a quarterly "pulse check" to gauge your progress. In order to compare apples to apples, quarter-to-quarter, and year-over-year, you must stick to the same set of questions. Here again, many companies change the survey questions each year, which makes it impossible to determine where progress is being made and what areas still need attention.

If the quarterly data is directionally correct, keep doing what you are doing, Champ. And, if the quarterly data shows that progress is not being made, you are still a Champ, but you need to ramp up your efforts. Schedule a Town Hall Meeting for every leader and people manager in your company, and have your CEO review your employee engagement strategy. Let people know they will be held accountable for their actions and results, and then follow through on your word.

Step 5: Hold People Managers Accountable

There is nothing more demoralizing to an employee than a management team who allows a person to stay in their role who is not pulling their weight, who has a toxic attitude, or who cannot effectively lead others. If you have a people manager who is unwilling or unable to execute on your employee engagement strategy, even after being coached, he/she should be terminated or moved to an individual contributor role. Your people managers are the frontline to your employees. Their leadership will make or break your ability to re-engage employees, so it's up to you to ensure they are doing what they are being paid to do.

If Not You, Who? was written for you. As a leader, your role is to step up and "own" employee engagement—to create an environment that people love where they can soar, so your company can soar.

THE TRUTH

Owning up to the responsibilities you have to the Earth—and the people you share it with—and making a difference in this world is the real definition of success.

Owning up to the responsibilities you have to the Earth—and the people you share it with—and making a difference in this world is the real definition of success. Nothing matters more and nothing will make you feel more fulfilled in life. It's why you were created. It's why you exist. It's part of your purpose.

Remember: *Everything rises and falls on leadership.* Everything. If a company has high levels of employee engagement and is meeting or exceeding its goals, odds are there's a great leader or leadership team that has owned up to its responsibilities.

By following the game plan above, Champ, you will create an environment that people love because it lights them up inside, and inspires them to give their all and then some. Tackle this issue with confidence, courage, presence, and optimism. Make your employee disengagement crisis a priority. When you do, you will see results. Your employees, customers, owners, and shareholders will be grateful they have a Champion in their midst. More importantly, you will have put your piece of the puzzle in place. Now that's what I call success. Kapow!

About the Author

Founder and President of Jill Christensen International, Jill is a genuine, direct, results-focused, high-energy leader.

Jill's career spans more than 25 years, where she has built a distinguished record of achievements. She led global internal communications teams at industry-leading Fortune 500 companies, including Avaya and Western Union. Jill has also advised executives, and directed communications and employee engagement programs in seven different industries, in companies such as AT&T, Lucent Technologies, Arrow, Novartis, TIAA-CREF, CSG International, Orica Mining, and the City & County of Denver.

An expert in employee engagement, Jill is a visionary change agent and dynamic speaker, with a bold self-confident leadership style. She has entertained, educated and inspired audiences for the past 15 years, speaking at Fortune 500 companies, industry conferences, the Conference Board in New York City and to MBA students at East Coast universities.

Jill has traveled the world in pursuit of new adventures, change and her innate desire to discover the unknown. She relocated to Denver from the East Coast in 2009, and is passionate about global travel, skiing, interior design, gardening, live music, extraordinary food and wine, American football, horse racing, volunteering, balance and Maine Coon cats.

Working With Jill

My greatest passion in life is fulfilling my purpose and helping others do the same. It lights me up inside to help leaders realize their potential, and create workplaces that people love, driving extraordinary levels of performance and profitability. Whether you are a global Fortune 500 corporation or a new business owner with a glimmer in your eye of what your small business could be, I offer:

- Keynote Speech and *If Not You, Who?* Book Signing
- Workshops and Breakout Sessions
- One-on-One Consulting

New services are added regularly, so please view my latest product suite at www.JillChristensenIntl.com.

Employee engagement is not hard. If you're committed, we can move mountains and crack the code of employee disengagement in your company. I've done it in large, global, complex, political organizations, so I know that together, we can do it in your company. I'd be honored to roll up my sleeves and partner with you to bring out your inner Champion and change the course of your company's destiny. Yes, employee engagement is that big.

Your employees, customers, owners, and shareholders will be grateful they have a true leader in their midst (you). More importantly, you will have put your piece of the puzzle in place. Now that's what I call success.

Call me...

Jill

+1 (303) 999-9224 | Jill@JillChristensenIntl.com |

JillChristensenIntl.com

JOIN ME! TWITTER, YOUTUBE, FACEBOOK, LINKEDIN, GOOGLE+

NOTES

_____

_____

_____

_____

_____

_____

_____

_____

_____

_____

_____

_____

_____

_____

_____

_____

_____

_____

_____

_____

_____

_____

_____

_____

NOTES

NOTES

_____

_____

_____

_____

_____

_____

_____

_____

_____

_____

_____

_____

_____

_____

_____

_____

_____

_____

_____

_____

_____

_____

_____

_____

_____

NOTES

NOTES

_____
_____
_____
_____
_____
_____
_____
_____
_____
_____
_____
_____
_____
_____
_____
_____
_____
_____
_____
_____
_____
_____
_____
_____
_____

NOTES

NOTES

_____

_____

_____

_____

_____

_____

_____

_____

_____

_____

_____

_____

_____

_____

_____

_____

_____

_____

_____

_____

_____

_____

_____

_____

NOTES

_____

_____

_____

_____

_____

_____

_____

_____

_____

_____

_____

_____

_____

_____

_____

_____

_____

_____

_____

_____

_____

_____

_____

NOTES

NOTES

NOTES

_____

_____

_____

_____

_____

_____

_____

_____

_____

_____

_____

_____

_____

_____

_____

_____

_____

_____

_____

_____

_____

_____

_____

_____

NOTES

_____
_____
_____
_____
_____
_____
_____
_____
_____
_____
_____
_____
_____
_____
_____
_____
_____
_____
_____
_____
_____
_____
_____

NOTES

_____

_____

_____

_____

_____

_____

_____

_____

_____

_____

_____

_____

_____

_____

_____

_____

_____

_____

_____

_____

_____

_____

_____

_____

_____

NOTES

_____

_____

_____

_____

_____

_____

_____

_____

_____

_____

_____

_____

_____

_____

_____

_____

_____

_____

_____

_____

_____

_____

NOTES

_____

_____

_____

_____

_____

_____

_____

_____

_____

_____

_____

_____

_____

_____

_____

_____

_____

_____

_____

_____

_____

_____

_____

NOTES

NOTES

NOTES

NOTES

_____

_____

_____

_____

_____

_____

_____

_____

_____

_____

_____

_____

_____

_____

_____

_____

_____

_____

_____

_____

_____

_____

_____

NOTES

NOTES

_____

_____

_____

_____

_____

_____

_____

_____

_____

_____

_____

_____

_____

_____

_____

_____

_____

_____

_____

_____

_____

_____

_____

_____